Treasures

of Worth

MOLLY HARVEY

~ A Pioneer Missionary ~

Treasures of Worth
Copyright © 1994 Molly Harvey

Printed by J. C. Print Ltd., Belfast

Copies from
Acre Gospel Mission
33 Ravensdene Park,
Belfast, BT6 ODA
Northern Ireland,
U.K.

or

Ambassador Production Ltd.,
16 Hillview Avenue,
Belfast, BT5 6JR
Northern Ireland,
U.K.

acre gospel mission   AMBASSADOR

Contents

acre gospel mission

working in

BRAZIL

PORTUGAL

CANARY ISLANDS

Acre Gospel Mission
33 Ravensdene Park,
Belfast, BT6 ODA
N. Ireland

Preface

Forty years ago in Bangor, Mollie Harvey held a group of young students spellbound as she recounted some of her experiences in Brazil. In our imagination we were there with her. Twelve years later I had the privilege of meeting up with Mollie in Boca do Acre and seeing some of the results of her work there. Today, in appreciation of all she did in that town, the Town council have named a local primary school "The Mary Harvey School" and pay the salaries of the church members who teach in it.

Twenty two years after she left Rio Branco, we, having just arrived in that town, wanted to buy a fridge but our money was delayed in Manaus - some 1200 miles away. The owner of the store agreed to accept a small deposit to secure the fridge for a few days- it was the last one in stock. From our difficulty with the language he knew that we were foreigners and enquired as to our origins. When we said Ireland he remarked that years ago he had known in Rio Branco a missionary from Ireland - a Miss Harvey, who indeed had delivered some of his children. On learning that we were connected with the same Mission, he insisted that we take immediate possession of it and to pay him whenever convenient. "It's all right if you are friends of Miss Mary," explained this man we had never met before.

Mollie is still remembered in Brazil with great affection and I know that you will enjoy reading her reflections in these pages.

Dr. Tom Geddis

Chapter One

❧

From The Beginning

"Miss Harvey, I doubt if you would be able to survive more than a year in such an inhospitable climate as the Amazon forests of Brazil. I don't think your heart would stand up to it. Besides, there would be very little medical help for you should you become ill."

That was the doctor's advice to me when I went for a medical prior to my first departure for Brazil in 1937. The old addage goes, " Doctors differ and patients die." This time the addage is reversed. Several doctors of that time agreed with this doctor's prognosis. Their counsel was given with the best intentions, but all those doctors are dead and I am still alive to tell the tale and and give testimony to God's glory almost sixty years later. Over thirty of these years were spent in that "inhospitable climate!"

I was born in Glasgow Scotland, but when I was eight years old, my father moved his position in work from Greenock in Renfrewshire, to a job at Mackies on the Springfield Road in Belfast. We went to live on the nearby Woodvale Road. That was a very big move in my life.

My sister, brother and I attended Woodvale School. Everything was new and I felt so lonely . It was then I met Margaret McKnight, who was a little older than me, but she and her sister became my friends and they were very helpful to me. Little did I know that Margaret would not only become my best friend, but also a lifelong colleague in the Lord's work.

After we left school to seek employment, we continued to meet with each other on the Shankhill Road. There was something about Margaret that made me want to be like her. She seemed to be always carrying her Bible and I would muse to myself, "I wonder where Margaret is going?" She often spoke to me about the Lord Jesus Christ, the Bible and my personal need of salvation. Margaret's witness convinced me that I was a sinner and whatever she had was what I needed. However, although I so wanted to be like her, the attractions of the world were already crowding into my life.

One dark and rainy night another friend came over to my house. We decided to go out walking on the Shankhill Road but because of the inclement weather we knew we would not be able to go very far. We then agreed to go down to the Albert Hall on the lower Shankhill and hear the renowned Irish evangelist, W. P. Nicholson. Although we both went to church on Sunday and attended a Bible Class, deep in my heart I knew I was living a false life and I longed to be better.

As Mr. Nicholson preached I realised I was a lost sinner. That night I went home but tossed and turned in the bed for I could not sleep. I knew something was wrong with me and I could hardly wait for the dawning of the day. It was only later I realised I had been under deep conviction of sin. I knew I must go back to those meetings and hear the evangelist again. The following night I not only returned to the mission,

I trusted the Lord Jesus as my Saviour. I was able then to truthfully sing, "What a wonderful change in my life has been wrought, since Jesus came into my heart." I felt as though I was walking on air as I went home to tell my mother. She, who was always in prayer for the family, was overjoyed. I am thankful that my mother did not give up praying for me.

The following Friday my friend and I went back to the mission but we could not get into the Albert Hall because of the crowd. We were about to leave when suddenly Margaret McKnight was by our side inviting us, "Come with me through the choir door and we will find seats." As we walked along she asked if we were saved, and , praise the Lord, we were able to tell her we were.

I remember Margaret asked where we were going to the next night and she invited us to go with her to the Northumberland Street Mission Hall on the Shankhill Road. We said we would love to go and made plans to meet her there. On that Saturday night Margaret waited for us at the door and when we arrived she led us in. This surely was a momentous step in the plan of my new-found Lord. His hand was leading one step at a time, even when I was not aware of it.

I will never forget that night. The Hall was packed with young men and women singing, "At the Cross, At the Cross, where I first saw the light, and the burden of my heart rolled away." A young man named Willie McComb was at the front leading the singing. I felt as though my heart would burst with love for Jesus Christ as I was able to sing those songs of testimony with true personal meaning for the first time.

Soon I was attending Mr. Flack's Bible Class on a Monday night and the missionary prayer meeting on Tuesdays. At these prayer meetings, missionaries came to tell of their work in different places around the world. One night a lady from Africa spoke. She was working with the World-wide Evangelisation Crusade (WEC) and told of the great need of thousands who had never heard the name of Jesus Christ. My heart was greatly touched.

Even as I was rejoicing that all my sins had been forgiven and that I was justified in God's sight, I felt the awesome responsibility of Christ's great commission, "Go ye into all the world and preach the Gospel to every creature." (Mark 16:15) Sitting in my seat, I quietly told the Lord I was willing to go wherever He wanted to send me. I was only a young girl. That night all else grew dim as my heart was set on the Lord's will. From that our time on the ambition of my life was to tell the glorious news of the Gospel to others.

That dear missionary never knew what had taken place in my life, but some day when we meet in heaven, I will thank her for sharing her vision and burden with us that night.

All else went dim,
My soul went after Him,
Would you not follow
If you heard Him call?

I began to attend the Northumberland Street Mission Hall, and it proved to be a wonderful training ground for me. I started taking part in many of the outreach activities of the Hall such as door-to-door visitation, teaching a Sunday School class and open-air evangelism. At first I was very shy. Speaking in public terrified me, but little by little the dear Lord helped me overcome my fears and in so doing I gained valuable experience for my missionary work in future years. I remember going to the Portstewart Convention, and, in the missionary meeting on Friday, as the appeal went forth for those who were willing to obey the Lord, I rose to my feet in response.

Soon after, I went to study at Redcliffe Missionary Training College in London to prepare myself for future work. Besides Bible training I felt that if I was going to help minister to all the needs of the people I would need to equip myself in nursing. I did my nursing training at the Mildmay Mission Hospital in London which was an invaluable experience and where I met some very dear friends. After completion of General nursing, I returned to Belfast and did the midwifery course at Malone Place in Belfast. These years of preparation proved to be a worthwhile investment of time medicine and midwifery as the keys to open many doors for the Gospel in far off Acre and Amazonas.

Chapter Two

❧

From A Humble Inception

Margaret McKnight had married the young man who led the choruses at the Northumberland Street Mission - Willie McComb. Together they had gone to Brazil to serve the Lord in 1925 and I became very interested in their work. After finishing my training at Bible College they were on furlough and as I listened to Willie and Margaret the Lord gave me a great burden for the people of Brazil. I knew the Lord wanted me to serve Him there. When the reality of such an expedition sank in, I was more than a little frightened. Nevertheless, I trusted the Lord and took one step at a time. Very soon the Lord opened the way and I felt I should join Willie and Margaret as a team returning to Brazil.

All of these steps were steps of faith and at times we dared to trust God for the impossible. As we went out we had no Mission structure behind us. God raised up men who promised to stand by the home end of the work while we went forth. They were like those who held ropes for Paul while he was let down the walls of Damascus. We thanked God for these faithful men who would form the basis of the Committee for what would become the Acre Gospel Mission. They, with us were prepared to trust God to supply all our needs according to the promises God had pledged to us in His Word.

Because we were going to a new pioneer area of Brazil and so far into the Amazon jungle, it was felt that I should have a medical check up. Initially the doctors thought I had a murmur in the heart and would not survive more than a year in such a tropical climate. I remember another Christian worker asking me to point out on a map where we were going. When he traced the place to so far up the Amazon he said, "Rather Willie McComb than me taking two ladies so far and to such a remote place." We were not foolhardy but we were clear of the God's call and stepped out on His promise and command.

For Willie and Margaret to return to Brazil they would have to leave behind their only child Irene, a lovely little girl just four and a half years old. In those days they felt it unwise to take her on such a journey into the unknown. Instead of going back to the lower Amazon, the Lord had placed a burden and a vision on Willie's heart for the people who lived in the Territory of Acre, two and a half thousand miles from the mouth of the mighty Amazon.

The Lord helped Willie and Margaret stand by that decision when a very kind school master and his wife, Mr. & Mrs. Evans of Ballywalter, offered to keep Irene while her parents were in Brazil for what was hoped to be a four or five year term. Mr. and Mrs. Evans had a little girl the same age as Irene and she was a great playmate for her.

One day Irene overheard her parents speaking to friends explaining why they felt it unwise to take her with them. She began questioning them each night as they prayed with her and put her to bed. Her question was always the same, "Daddy, Mummy, you wouldn't go away and leave me, would you?" Not wanting to lie to their little daughter, they had to run out of the room to shed their own tears.

Finally the day of departure came, and as a parting gift, her parents bought her a lovely doll which they gave her as she was leaving for Ballywalter. With her attention wrapped up in the new dolly, the car door shut and Irene was away. That day I was glad I was not married. The sight of the car going down the road into the distance would be relived many times, for that was the last sight Willie and Margaret had of Irene for eight and a half long years. Their plans for a shorter term in Brazil were to be dashed by the outbreak of war.

June 4th., 1937 was the date set for Willie, Margaret and me to start our long journey to the far off Acre Territory of Brazil. I can still remember the cabin trunk, suit cases and bed bag all piled up in the hallway of our home. Although it was summer time , the morning was dull and wet and not helpful for a family parting.

My dear father did not go to work that day. He stood looking out of the sitting room window waiting for the man to come for the baggage. The person we were waiting for attended the meetings at Northumberland Street and had offered to transport the baggage for the missionaries and spare the extra expense. Eventually he arrived with his horse and cart, and as the rain pelted down, saturating the already wet cart, we loaded on all the baggage. My father kept saying that everything was getting soaked, but the poor man did not have a cover for the cart. After loading all my earthly goods on his cart, the man with his horse and cart left our house and went for Willie and Margaret's baggage.

It was a full day's work to have all the baggage transported to the Liverpool boat at the Donegall Quay in Belfast and after all was loaded we also embarked on the steamer for the crossing to England on the first leg of our long sea journey.

The fare to Brazil cost eighteen pounds per person, plus one pound for our passports! We also had to pay our fares to Liverpool but we travelled on the economic second class. That was a lot of money during the days of extreme hardship before World War II. However, we were sure God had called us and He would never fail to supply our need. All the expenses of that initial journey to Brazil were fully met by a sacrificial gift of £100 from two elderly ladies from Portrush.

I shall never forget the crowd that gathered at the docks that night to see us off. There were hundreds of the Lord's people from different churches and mission halls. Among the many friends who gathered at the docks that night was the Chairman of the newly formed Acre Committee, Pastor Olley of Newtownards Baptist Church. Many members of his church were in the crowd, including a teenage girl who stood beside my parents. As she stood there that teenage girl made a vow that she would pray for the three of us every day. That young, dedicated, girl was Dorric Cavan who would become Dorrie Gunning. Little did we know then that one day she, and her husband James, would also be farewelled from the same docks on their way to the very region for which we were bound.

As we stood on the cold grey deck waves of many mixed emotions were continually washing over us. We were sad to leave our loved ones and our wonderful Ulster with its many friends, but we were also excited to be on our way and impatient to reach our destination.

As the Liverpool steamer sounded its horn the shrill sound of which echoed around the quayside, the gathered crowd sang missionary hymns of farewell and encouragement. Some shouted out promises from God's Word. Others waved their handkerchiefs as their final farewell. As I looked back on the receding dockside I wondered how many of our dear friends we would not meet again on earth. Little did we know that within the span of three short years Willie, Margaret and myself would each have one of our parents pass away to be with Christ.

The journey to Brazil was quite uneventful except for a few storms which blew butterflies into my stomach. The fifteen day voyage was not long going in as I practiced my smattering of Portuguese on the passengers from Brazil and Portugal. After our arrival at the mouth of the Amazon we travelled for six weeks up the winding Amazon River to Manaus on a flat bottomed, wood burning river steamer. We had to stop every three days to take on a fresh supply of logs for fuel.

After Manaus we continued travelling west up the main artery of the Amazon, the river Solimoes, and then entered another great tributary, the river Purus, and headed slowly up river in a southwesterly direction for over a thousand miles to Rio Branco, the capital of Acre.

On our way up river we passed dozens of small towns and villages without a gospel witness and in the last thousand five hundred miles, we never met one evangelical missionary. During the six weeks on the river and wherever we stopped, Willie McComb sold Bibles and distributed gospel literature. He was always buying up the opportunities to witness for the Lord. He even had occasion to witness to the captain of the vessel on which we were travelling. Everywhere we went we found, that in spite of the remoteness of the region, there was great hunger for the Word of God and an equally great open door for the preaching of the Gospel.

Chapter Three

❧

From Great Dangers

On disembarking at Rio Branco we faced many initial problems, some foreseen and others for which we could never have prepared for. Because this was a pioneer step we had no home to go to and no one to welcome us. For the first few days we had to make do with a dirty and bug invested hotel which charged exorbitant prices. The cost of living was extremely high and houses to rent were scarce, but the Lord provided one for us on the outskirts of the town. It was a wooden structure with a zinc roof which made the house very hot. This house was not only our residence, but also it was in this house we started our first meetings in Rio Branco. Very soon over fifty people packed into the front room and on the veranda. Our first converts in Acre came to the Lord in this house.

God's work is never easy nor does it run smoothly. There are always surprises and at times disappointments. However, God often uses these experiences to teach us to trust Him more and to accomplish His own purpose. The first major blow to us came when after only a few months renting this first house we were given two weeks notice to find somewhere else. We sensed the devil was opposing us each step of the way, but we were also aware that our great Provider went before us.

Willie McComb made contact with a Syrian whom we had met on the boat on our way to Rio Branco. He rented to us a much larger house in a more central location which gave us greater accommodation. Besides being our home, the gospel meetings continued to be held in this house for quite a while and still more people were added to the Lord. At the start we had only a few hymn books. Soon we had new books printed and Margaret and I stitched them together. These were to do us all our time in Rio Branco!

With a growing congregation, it soon became evident that we would need a proper church building. In the Lord's time we were enabled to purchase a house and the believers rallied round to renovate it into a meeting place. By sacrificial and voluntary labour they converted the dwelling from a three roomed house into a smartly painted church meeting place. A believer offered us wood from a rubber plantation and the believers sawed these trees into planks and made their own benches for use in the church.

Even though it was the State Capital, living conditions in Rio Branco were very basic. There were no cars or any form of motorized transport in the town. Bicycles also were unknown in Rio Branco. A lot of people rode horses in town which gave the impression of an American wild west town. Some streets had cobble stone paving but most were either dusty or muddy lane ways. Electricity was undependable as often the town's generator would be broken. There was no tap for running water. Instead, there was a very deep well at the back of the house.

There were many outstanding experiences during our eight years in Rio Branco. Some were delightful and others were horrific. It was a joy when Willie and Margaret had an addition to their family, another little girl whom they named Eleanor. She was a blessing to the home and a source of constant amusement and attention.

However, one day she gave us all a fright. The family who had lived in the rented house before us made some renovations to the building and the grounds. The father had built a brick wall around the well. The wall was about one foot thick and two feet high. Over the opening he had placed a wooden cover. It was the general custom to use clean five gallon kerosene tins as buckets to draw water. These were attached to a strong rope and lowered into the dark depths of the well and hauled up again full of water. The water was then taken to the kitchen or to the bathroom as needed. In the kitchen the water had to be strained and boiled. It was then divided into two containers; one held water used for cooking and the remainder of the water was tediously filtered for drinking.

One day when little Eleanor was about three years old, after drawing water from the well, someone had forgotten to replace the heavy cover over the well. Margaret, who had been working in the kitchen, looked out the kitchen door and saw that Eleanor had climbed up and was standing on the brick surround of the deep well. As Eleanor gazed into the well, she shouted to us that she could see herself in the water.

I heard a terrible scream from the kitchen as Margaret realized the danger to her daughter. The scream made me look out of the window and I saw the girl happily looking down into the dangerously fascinating well. I quickly pulled Margaret back into the kitchen; then I rushed to a shelf where I got some biscuits from a tin and very slowly walked outside and over to the well repeating, "Stand still Eleanor, I am coming with biscuits." As she turned to take the biscuit from me I threw my arms around her and placed her safely on the ground away from the danger of the murky depths of the well. I was trembling and my heart felt sore at the thought of what might have happened if she had heard her mother screaming. She would have most certainly jumped in fright or turned around, and I fear she would have lost her balance and plunged to her death in the well.

Not long after our nearly disastrous accident with Eleanor, I also was put through an ordeal which nearly proved fatal. The tropical rain had poured down all day. Those who had come to the Sunday morning service had arrived with wet clothes, and by evening it was still raining. All the roads were flooded so there was no evening service.

Willie, Margaret and little Eleanor were in their room, and I was sitting at the table in the dining room. I had my English Bible and Redemption hymn book in front of me. As I read Psalm 71, the first four verses seemed to grip my attention. Verse two reads, "Deliver me and cause me to escape." Then I noticed verse four, "Deliver me out of the hand of the unrighteous and cruel man." I really believed that God was telling me something. Could this be a warning to me?

As I sat at the table contemplating the reading, there came the sound of someone clapping their hands loudly outside our door. Our simple homes had no door bells or knockers; therefore, a visitor would simply clap his hands to announce his arrival. I wondered who might be outside. For some weeks I had been attending to a very nice little woman, Myrtle, who was expecting her first baby, and I figured I must be needed at her home. Sure enough, standing there in the pouring rain was her husband. He apologized for having to call me out on such a terrible night, but I did not mind. I soon gathered my medicine bag and followed him through the floods to his house.

I was there for several hours and the baby girl was born at 1.00 a.m.. She was their first baby, and they were delighted. We all then enjoyed a cup of coffee and a rest before the new father escorted me back to my house. I noticed that he was carrying a rather heavy stick, and although I thought this a bit unusual, I did not ask any questions. I figured he had seen a snake when he had come to call me.

The following week he told me had had brought a stick with him because he had felt someone watching us as I attended to his wife Myrtle. This was quite possible as the house was very open, only being enclosed halfway up the wall and the bed room the only room which was enclosed completely.

By the time I arrived home, the rain had stopped, but the slippery mud made the road treacherous. I came into the house as quietly as possible using only my flashlight so as not waken the others. Soon after taking my muddy shoes off, I again could hear someone on the veranda making a terrible noise, clapping and calling out for me. I tried to calm and hush him. I asked, "Is it Myrtle again; whatever is wrong?" By this time all the noise had wakened Margaret, and she told Willie I was called out to see Myrtle again. Like me, she was sure it was Myrtle's husband. But this time, we both were wrong.

I went out to the end of the veranda where I saw a tall Bolivian Indian. He had his head and face almost concealed

23

behind a grey blanket, and in the darkness of the early morning, I could not see him very well. He seemed quite nervous as he asked me to come quickly to his wife who was having their fifth child and there were complications. Because I did not know him, I asked him why he had not contacted me earlier about his wife's pregnancy. His answer was that they had come to live in Rio Branco only a short time ago. Even after his explanation, I was still wary of him. I asked him how he knew I was a midwife and how he knew where I lived. He told me, "Dona Gertrude told me about you, and she said you would come at once."

Dona Gertrude was a believer and a member of our church. She was a widow with a large family, and she attended and assisted many ladies at the time of their delivery. For this reason we knew her as "the handywoman."

One particular day not long before this, as I was passing her house, I stopped in for a chat, and she told be about a difficult birth she was worried about. I told her never to hesitate to call me at any hour of the night or day, and I would gladly come to help her. Little did I know that this Bolivian was in her house talking to her son at that time and had heard every word that was spoken. Unsuspecting of any danger, I prepared to follow him to help, as I thought, Dona Gertrude. But Dona Gertrude knew nothing about this Indian, who in all truthfulness had neither wife nor children.

I told the man to wait outside as I went back to get my midwifery bag. I was soon ready and we were off. The rain was still holding off, and we began the hazardous walk, slipping and sliding down the muddy road to the bridge. Because of the heavy rain that had fallen all the previous day, the water was rushing angrily under the bridge. At times I thought that the water would wash the little bridge away.

As I walked on to the bridge, the Indian caught my arm and said, "No, come this way." I knew the place well and knew that the way he was pulling me led only down to the river Acre. I then realized my suspicions had been well grounded, and that this man only had evil intentions; I began pulling one way and he the other. As we struggled in the darkness, he pulled my midwifery bag from me and threw it into the raging river. He then grabbed the flashlight from my hands and began smashing it into my face. Thankfully he did not have any other weapon, but with this flashlight, he managed to smash out several of my teeth and badly injure my left eye.

I know without a doubt that God was my Help and Deliverance that night. As I desperately struggled for my life, God gave me strength. The Indian was very tall whereas my height was only five feet, but I managed to thwart his evil intentions. His hands went round my throat and he began choking me; but for some reason he changed his mind. He dragged me, fighting all the way, to the side of the bridge and threw me over. As the dark swirling water engulfed me, I thought I was dead, but this was part of God's plan. The cold water shocked me back into action, and although I was already tired from the struggle, I floated in the stream. As I was swept down river by the rushing current, I was too tired to swim, and I thought I would be carried all the way out into the main flow of the river Acre. Suddenly my arm brushed against the stump of a tree, and I held on with all my strength.

Immediately I heard my attacker crashing through the brush at the edge of the river, and for the first time I began to cry out, "Help, somebody help me." I called urgently as I saw the Indian coming closer; I saw that he now had something in his hand, perhaps a tree branch, with which to strike my arm and loosen my grip, but by this time the new day was dawning, and my cries for help were heard. He hesitated for a moment then he dropped the stick and ran away over the bridge in the opposite direction as he had heard some one running toward the bridge.

Away up the hill there was a small house in which two young soldiers were living. They were to be on duty at four in the morning and were getting ready to leave when they heard my cries for help. They could tell someone was in trouble because of the tone of my voice, but I was so scared I didn't realise I was calling out in English and they didn't understand what I was calling. As they drew near I could hear one soldier say to another, "Could it be the missionary midwife in trouble? Perhaps there is a snake or a wild animal on the path." When they reached the bridge, they looked over and saw me in the water. They jumped into the swift flowing current and reached me just as I thought I could hold on no longer. They pulled me to the river bank and supported me as we made our way back up the hill toward the mission house. I had been in the cold water so long that my legs felt numb, and when I tried to walk on my bare feet, I felt as though I was walking on tiny pieces of glass.

Willie and Margaret got a rude awakening as we arrived on the veranda. I was soaking wet, and by this time my left eye was swelling shut and my mouth was still bleeding where my teeth had been knocked out. Margaret, thinking I had gone back to Myrtle's, told the soldiers that Myrtle's husband had been the one that had done this to me. Of course, the poor man knew nothing about what had happened and must have been terrified when the soldiers pulled him from his house and accused him of attacking me. When I heard what was happening, I was able to tell them the true story. We asked him to come to the house, and we explained the error and told him how his name had wrongly got mixed up in this incident. He was very understanding and very relieved.

Soon news of the attack reached the Chief of Police and the governor of the Acre Territory. Both were very annoyed that this had happened to a foreigner in their country. They had the two worst criminals in Rio Branco brought to my room where I was recovering. The first was a small man who wept when he saw me. The second, without doubt, was the Bolivian Indian who had called me out on that terrible night. He was very nervous and would not even look at me. The Chief of Police was there, and he saw the recognition on my face even before I said, "Yes, this is the man."

The Indian certainly had chosen a good night to attack me. There was so much mud on the roads that our tracks soon oozed in to oblivion, and because of the weather, there was no one out to witness the deed. But there was one witness, our Heavenly Father, Who neither slumbers nor sleeps. I had been delivered "out of the hand of the unrighteous and cruel man," and He had caused me to escape. This was the Psalm I had been reading before I went out on that dreadful Sunday night. My heart cried out for the souls of the wicked men who needed to be delivered from the power of the Devil whom they serve. I longed that they would come to find new life in Jesus Christ Who is the only One Who can give them power to overcome temptations. We all felt led not to pursue the matter any further.

Months later when the mail from home arrived, I received a letter which deeply touched me and proved to me how much a sincere and loving prayer partner can mean to a missionary on the mission field. The letter to which I refer came from Maria Hangarter who had trained as a nurse with me at Mildmay Hospital in London. When I was leaving for Brazil, she vowed to faithfully pray for me, and I know she did. In her letter she asked,, "What was wrong on January 23?" She had been awakened from sleep in a great fright, and there followed a great burden for me. The burden was so great that she fell down on her knees at her bedside and cried to the Lord. She wrote that she was soaked with her own sweat as she prayed. Some reading this might think she had been through a nightmare, but I believe that she was heard by our loving Heavenly Father, and my life was saved that very night. I know that no danger can so come near the Christian that He cannot intervene.

If you are a prayer partner, please never forget to pray, but rather continue constantly in prayer for the missionaries and their children who may be in great danger. Matthew 10:29 reminds us of God's care for the sparrows; and then verse thirty one continues "Ye are of more value than many sparrows." We have certainly proved this promise over and over again in our lives.

Chapter Four

❧

In From The Fields Of Labour

"If thou shalt do this thing, and God command thee so, then thou shalt be able to endure, and all this people shall also go to their place in peace." (Exodus 18:23)

We had wakened to a dark wet day. We were leaving Rio Branco, the capital of Acre, and the converts whom we dearly loved, having lived amongst them for eight and a half years. We had seen so many of them kneel and accept the Lord's offer of salvation and humbly give their lives to follow Him. We had seen them in their joys and sorrows. God had given us great love for them, but this day we were saying, "Goodbye."

They stood there on the muddy river bank in bare feet, with bare arms and legs and straggled hair, getting soaked as the heavy rain pelted down on them. We were on board a small river boat that would take us two and a half thousand miles down river to the city of Belem at the mouth of the Amazon; where on arrival there we hoped to get a boat sailing for England.

As the horn blew its "ready to move," we heard many lovely promises from the Scriptures being shouted to us from the believers. Tears were in our eyes as we watched the boat slip further and further away from them, but the further this boat moved down river, the more I knew in my heart that one day I would return to Acre. This was the beginning of our long journey home.

World War II was over, and many missionaries, not being able to travel during the war, were returning home. Willie and Margaret McComb were very lonely for their elder daughter, Irene, who had been left behind at home eight and a half years before. Now they were taking another daughter, five year old Eleanor, home for the first time.

From Rio Branco to the mouth of the Amazon is a long tiresome journey in a small boat. On reaching the coast and the city of Belem we found there was no hope of any boats taking passengers to England. In Belem we found accommodation and Willie went to the port every day to enquire if there was any ship bound for England. We prayed and we waited.

One day he came back very excited and told us to get our things packed again as we were going to New York on a Polish cargo vessel. He had spoken to the captain, and the captain had offered to take us to New York for a very small sum of money. Needless to say we were all delighted at this answer to prayer. We boarded the vessel the next day as it was sailing that afternoon. The captain was a gentleman and treated us very kindly, as did the crew. Although the sea was very rough all the way to America, the trip was not terribly unpleasant because we knew we were going home at last.

Near to the Island of Trinidad, in the Caribbean, we were caught in the throes of a dying hurricane. The captain ordered us into our cabins where we were locked in for our own safety. The boat was tossed about by mountainous waves as if it had been an old oak leaf at the mercy of a rushing river. I must admit I was very concerned when I saw some of the heavy deck cargo being thrown overboard into the angry sea. But, just as the storm ceased when Jonah was thrown into the sea, our hurricane soon diminished to only a tropical storm and then died completely.

After two weeks we arrived in New York. Quite a crowd was there awaiting our arrival, and as the ship sailed in, the people were cheering. They seemed to be happy to see the ship safely in port even without much of the heavy cargo, which by this time must been lying half covered in sand and silt at the bottom of the sea. Unknown to us, news had been given on American radio about the ship being in difficulty and having to jettison their cargo at sea to save the ship and passengers.

Once on terra firma, we were advised to immediately place our names on the waiting list for a passage to England, which we did. Happily, because we had been so long in the tropics, we were told that our names would be at the top of the waiting list in the shipping office. We then took a train to Canada to stay with Mrs. McComb's sister and family near Toronto. They received us warmly and we had a very welcome rest.

After we had been in Canada for a month or so, a telegram came one night at 10.00 p.m. giving us the good news that passages had been granted to us on the "HMS Queen Elizabeth," and we were to be on board the ship next day at noon. We praised the Lord for answering both our prayers and those of the caring Acre Committee in Belfast.

We rushed around packing our cases and were ready for the midnight train from Toronto to New York. The train was so full that many of us had to sit on our cases for most of the journey, but some kind folks shared their seats with us during the night. The train reached New York in good time, and when we arrived in the harbour, I can remember feeling quite dizzy as I looked up at the height of that wonderful ship, the "HMS Queen Elizabeth." It was not as posh as before the war, because it had been used as a troop carrier during the years of combat. Once on board, I was placed in a cabin with eight other ladies. There were two thousand passengers on board which included people from all classes and walks of life. Hundreds of them had been just been released from prisoner of war camps in Japan. Many of these still looked ill but were well cared for on the journey by the male nurses and doctors who accompanied them.

The voyage home was long and tiresome, but we did not mind for we were going home to friends and relatives who had only been memories for more than eight years. Finally we arrived and disembarked in Southhampton. Again, thousand were gathered at the docks. The cheers were thunderous. The prisoners were home at last! In some aspects the war had made prisoners of us all since we could neither come nor go from our respective lands. "Land of Hope and Glory" was never sung with such gusto as was reverberated from shore to shore at the harbour on that fine day. Many missionaries were welcomed by loved ones. At the call of the King of Kings, they had gone to distant lands before the war started and each could tell of precious souls they had seen delivered from darkest paganism to a new life in our wonderful Saviour, the Lord Jesus Christ.

At Southampton we boarded a train for Euston Station in London. The weather was extremely cold, and were informed that no train was leaving for Liverpool until next evening at 6.00 p.m. Just as we had begun to look for accommodation, right outside the station, we found an old lady who offered us two attic rooms in an apartment house. I think we would have been thankful for a hole in the ground to get out of the bitterly cold station, and we were indeed very grateful for the nice warm rooms.

The next morning at breakfast she told us that many policemen were lined up outside her door in Euston Square. We knew that this meant some member of the Royal Family was arriving on one of the trains and if we stood on the steps outside, we would probably manage to see them. Soon we heard cheering from down the street, and the sound became louder and louder until it was a roar as Queen Elizabeth and the two princesses passed by in a beautiful open carriage. The Queen must have noticed this little fair haired jumping bean and bent forward a little and waved back at her. Little did Her Majesty know how far this little child had travelled, and on this her first day on English soil Eleanor got this wave of the hand from the Queen of England!

The following day we went by train to Liverpool where we boarded the Belfast Steamer for home. We were given a lovely welcome at the shore, and waiting there was Margaret and Willie's daughter, Irene, who had been left in Ulster so many years before. The small girl who did not want her parents to go, was now a tall teenager, apprehensive and unsure of how to greet those who had been dear memories for these eight childhood years and now they had materialized into hugging parents. How wonderfully kind Mr. & Mrs. Evans of Ballywalter had been to her all those years.

Although there were many tearful and happy reunions, many of those who had waved us off to Brazil were now with the Lord. Each of us had lost one of our parents. Margaret's mother, Willie's father and my father had all gone to be with Christ. It is wonderful to know that I shall meet them all again in heaven.

It was good to be home with the loving family circle. The prayers of God's dear people had been answered. He had not failed us.

> *Through many dangers, toils and snares*
> *We have already come,*
> *'Tis grace that brought us safe thus far,*
> *And grace will lead us home.*

Chapter Five

❧

From Rio Branco To Sena Madureira

After a relaxing and yet busy furlough during which I had good times with my family, and with friends and supporters of the Acre Gospel Mission in churches, mission halls and many homes, I felt the time was right to return to Brazil. I told Mr. & Mrs. McComb of my plans. They knew I had promised the believers in Acre that I would return. I then approached the Mission Committee for their advice and, hopefully, their consent.

They were pleased and yet somewhat cautious that I was returning alone. They were not in favour of my going back to Rio Branco where I had worked for the previous eight years because it was in that town I had been attacked by the Bolivian Indian. Due to the fact that no one witnessed his attack, he was a free man walking the streets of the town. In light of this, the Committee members felt this could be a danger and they advised me to seek God's will about going to another town in Acre. I agreed to seek an answer from God about this.

One day as I was praying and asking for guidance, God gave me a promise from Isaiah 45:2-3, "I will go before thee, and make the crooked places straight; I will break in pieces the gates of brass, and cut in sunder the bars of iron; and I will give thee the treasures of darkness and hidden riches of secret places, that thou mayest know that I the Lord which call thee by thy name, am the God of Israel."

Just at this time I was invited to visit a young couple, James and Dorrie Gunning, in the town of Newtownards. They were not many years married and had a lovely home. They told how they knew without a doubt that the Lord had called them to His work in Acre and they had already approached the committee about going with the Acre Gospel Mission. Soon after this, they went into training at the Bible Training Institute in Glasgow and after completion of their course were accepted for the work in Acre. They were to follow me later to Brazil. Little did any of us know that this young couple, which the committee had accepted, would serve the Lord under the Acre Gospel Mission for forty two years in Brazil and be loved by all whom they served.

From the day I left Belfast in June 1947, travelling as a single lady, until I arrived in the city of Manaus many weeks later, the Lord helped me get through every day, one by one. When I reached Manaus and was able to clear customs, the Lord's provision for me was a lovely surprise. Willard and Grace Stull, American missionaries whom I had first known since coming to Brazil in 1937, were home on furlough and knowing I was coming to Manaus, they had left me the key to their furnished house for my use as long as I would need it.

During my time in Manaus I was much in prayer as to where the Lord would have me go to work for Him in Acre. I was attending a church in the city and had begun to know the members. One day I had opportunity to share with the church that I was on my way to Acre, and one nice couple told me they had lived and worked in Acre for years. They had lived in the town of Sena Madureira. They said that there was a missionary there, but he was leaving soon to go back to go back to see his family in Norway. Sander Tonnesson was a Norwegian and had not seen his family since the beginning of World War II. He had stayed with Mr. & Mrs. McComb in Rio Branco for some time. After that he and another Norwegian missionary went to Sena Madureira. I listened with interest to all that they told me about this new town and I began to wonder if this could be the town to which the Lord would have me go. I believed this was God's first witness to me about a new opening, but I wanted to be sure, and I asked God to confirm this to me.

The house I was staying in was just across the road from a corner on which there was a medical clinic. Every day crowds of people gathered to see a doctor and receive treatment. Old fashioned open tram-cars, passed up and down the road each day and brought patients from all over Manaus. I had been watching one old lady who came out of the clinic and stood in the hot sun. She would try to cover her eyes with her hand as she stood waiting for the tram-car. One day I could stand it no longer, and I went over to her and asked her to come over to the house for a cup of coffee and a chat.

She told me she went to the clinic every day to get drops in her eyes, and with tears she told she was sure she was going blind. When I looked at her eyes I saw she had a cataract in both eyes. I asked her where she lived, and to my great surprise she told me she lived in Acre in a town called Sena Madureira. She also told me that her daughter was a believer and that she knew the missionary there and his meetings were very good.

When I told her I was planning on going to Acre as soon as the water level rose on the River Purus (the water level had been too low for boats for a few months) she was delighted and said, "Oh will you take me to Acre with you after I have the operation on my eyes? Please come to Sena with me!" Of course, I could make no promise yet, but I felt that this was the Lord's confirmation that I had been seeking. However, I was still not sure, and I prayed like Gideon prayed long ago - that God would not to be angry for asking for another sign .

Not long after, I received a letter from Sander Tonnesen who was soon to leave Sena Madureira to return to Norway. He had heard I was in Manaus, and, in his letter, was asking me to pray much about coming to the work of the Lord in Sena Madureira. He finished the letter by saying that the church members had been much in prayer and were awaiting an answer. Here was the third and final confirmation, and it was with a joyful heart that I thanked the Lord for confirming His call so definitely.

I wrote back to Sander and the believers in Sena Madureira telling them I felt it was the Lord's will for me to accept their invitation. Sander and the church members were delighted at my reply.

Isaiah 30:21, "And thine ears shall hear a word behind thee, saying, This is the way, walk ye in it, when ye turn to the right hand, and when ye turn to the left." I now had peace in my heart. It was to Sena Madureira that I was appointed to go.

I boarded the steamer in Manaus and got the dear old lady safely on with me. The crew were so good to her and to me during the weeks we were on that steamer. Over all the years I travelled long distances, and often alone, on river boats of the "Amazon Steamship Company," never once did I ever find the crew offensive. They always treated me with the utmost respect and for that I was always grateful.

After changing to a smaller craft in Boca do Acre, we headed up the river Purus and then into the river Iaco. There was great excitement when we got our first sight of Sena Madureira.

Sander Tonnesen, with many members of the church, were at the port to meet us. They came on board and we had a great welcome from all. The old lady had travelled well and she was delighted to see her daughter who was a new convert in the church.

One lady, Dona Maria Morena, invited us from the boat to her house for a welcome cup of coffee. From there we had to go to another house where another couple had prepared dinner for us. This was the home of Sr. Valdimar and Dona Esther who had two daughters and a son. I was told that they had used their home for Sunday morning meetings and they had one room set aside as "father's prayer room ."

After a sumptuous dinner I was taken down the main street of the town and shown the church and right next to it, the house belonging to the church where I would stay. One of the believers offered to send his daughter to live with me. Her name was Corina. She was a gem of a girl and would remain with us for years. When James and Dorrie arrived, she went to live with them and was as close to them as a daughter. All our missionaries in Brazil loved Corina and we were heart broken years later when she tragically died in another remote part of the Amazon while travelling with her husband.

Before Sander left for Norway, he, with other members of the church, took me to visit believers who lived in the forest around Sena Madureira, These visits involved crossing rivers or slippery bridges, and walking for hours through dense jungle, to reach the homes of these believers. We were always greeted with a lovely meal. This was followed with a meeting at which all the neighbouring forest dwellers were invited to attend. These were memorable visits and it was great for me to meet the Christians. Today in many isolated places the believers have their own small churches.

Many times while returning from the trek to distant places, I felt so happy and yet humbled that God had chosen me to serve Him amongst these dear people. Even as I think of them now I find myself singing,

> *"I have only one life on this earth,*
> *And as vapour it is passing away.*
> *We must labour for treasures of worth*
> *Ere toil ends at the close of of day*
>
> *Only one life and white is the field,*
> *With compassion this great need I view.*
> *This one life that I have, I will yield,*
> *And the little that I can do.*
>
> *Only one life to give*
> *I must never withhold it from God*
> *Only one life to live,*
> *I must not miss the "Well done" from God.*

Chapter Six

❧

A Brand From The Burning

February had arrived and with it came the rain - in fact, this was the height of the wet season. The small house in which I was living had a kitchen at the back which, because of dampness, had a rotten floor, and I was afraid of falling through it any day! I had bought several dozens of ten-foot boards with which to fix it as I had received word that James and Dorrie had been accepted by the Mission Committee and were coming out to join me in the work. I knew they had already left Belfast and had begun the long journey out to Brazil. I was very pleased that they were coming to work with me in Sena Madureira.

I had leaned the boards against the side of house to dry before the carpenter commenced his work. Alas, the tropical rain poured down daily and the boards were sodden. As the rains continued, the roads began to flood, and we watched helplessly as the river Iaco rose higher and higher. Finally the banks of the river could contain the rushing torrent no longer. The river overflowed its banks and swept into the town with an unstoppable resolution causing a terrible flood. One morning I woke to the strange sound of something gurgling and swishing in my room. Upon stepping from the bed, I found myself standing in dirty river water which was pouring in to the house. By this time the water was ankle deep, and each hour it was rising higher.

Two of the elders from the church told me I would have to use the boards, which I had bought to fix the kitchen floor, to make a raised platform on which the trunks, camp beds, furniture, etc. could be placed out of the damaging reach of the ever-rising water. So they started to saw into smaller pieces the long fine boards, and when they finished the platform, up on top went everything we considered valuable. By this time we were wading around the house in river water up to our knees.

The church building next door had been newly painted a nice shade of cream for the arrival of the new missionaries. But now it was flooded in three feet of dirty water which left a reminding mark on the walls for many years.

It soon became necessary for me to move to higher ground so I went to stay with a dear Christian widow who lived away up the side of a hill. I noticed how large her front room was, and upon my remarking on this, she gladly gave us permission to conduct the Lord's Day and Tuesday night meetings in her home. Because the water was so deep on the roads the believers had to use their canoes to transport the benches, two at a time, to the house loaned to us by the lady. It was quite a job as they transported everything, even the small organ out of the church, to a dry area and then had to carry the things up the hill to this large room. The room was soon ready for the meetings, and we were all very happy.

The believers who lived in the town had to paddle in their canoes for part of the way and then walk up the hill for the meetings while those living nearby found things much easier. In spite of the flood, the Lord blessed, and many strangers attended our makeshift church on the hill. We had only paraffin-oil lamps, and most of the believers brought their own little lamps made out of condensed milk tins. The room was soon dimmed with the smoke, and although our eyes got red and sore, the smoke did not seem to deter the bloodthirsty mosquitoes. This proved to be a difficult time for us, but our loving heavenly Father had His eye upon us , and He was working out His own divine purpose as we soon learned.

Senhor Joao Marinho, infamously known in the town as the enemy of the Gospel, had to pass this very house on the hill in order to get to his home. His own little house was located far back in the forest. He was one of the men who had come to the Acre as a rubber cutter from Rio Grande do Norte. Joao was an ardent Roman Catholic who hated believers. He would often come to the door of the church, and whether we were singing hymns or preaching the Gospel, he would stand looking in and at the same time blocking his ears with his fingers. He wanted to know who was in the meeting and many of the believers were afraid of him. With the town being flooded as well as the house and church, we had now come to this house to preach and sing and it was on the very road that led to his house. He was amazed, if not angry, for in the stillness of the forest the singing of the gospel hymns could be heard for miles around and even in Joao's own house.

Then one Sunday morning as Joao was walking past the house, he halted on the road, came a little nearer and looked in. Sunday School was in progress for children and adults aged from eight to eighty, and all were eagerly learning the Scriptures. I was at the front telling the story of Joseph with the aid of the large flannel-graph pictures. I noticed Joao at the open door, and seeing him there caused me to begin praying as well as teaching. We always left a few seats vacant at the back of the church, and we did the same in this house. One of our older deacons went to the door, pointed to the seat and very graciously invited Joao to come in and sit down. He did just that, and I went on with the story telling how God had been with Joseph even through his hard times. Joao told me later that as he sat and looked at me, he said to himself, "I don't believe that person is telling lies, because I have heard this same story before."

Oh, how those dear Brazilian folk could teach some of us. If they were somewhat afraid or suspicious of him, they did not show it. They did not turn to stare, nor did they whisper to their neighbour. In fact, they went to him, men and women, shook his hand and told him how glad they were to see him. He asked, "May I come again tonight?" We assured him he could, and he did return. Sander Tonnesen the Norwegian missionary who had now returned, was the speaker that evening. He gave a clear Gospel message that night, and in my memory I can still see him speaking at the front - Bible in one hand and a little paraffin lamp giving off black smoke, in the other, but the presence of the Lord was real, and all the believers were quietly praying for this poor misled and unhappy man sitting in the back seat. At the end of the service the mixed choir sang in Portuguese,

"Christ for me, Christ for me,
From all the fear of what men think or say,
Christ for me."

Joao asked if he could have further instruction as we did not press for a response to the invitation given at he close of the meeting. We did not want to pluck unripe fruit and therefore Sander arranged to meet him the following night. The next night Sander made clear to Joao the way of salvation and he gave his heart to the Good Shepherd.

He was made a new creature in Christ Jesus by faith in our dear Saviour alone. This man who in the past had walked in his bare bleeding feet over stony ground for days in an attempt to atone for his sins, was now rejoicing in the freedom from his sins. From that day Joao's great desire was to go to his old companions and relatives with the Good News. I know of no other Brazilian believer who suffered so much as Joao did as he went in search of the other lost sheep. Joao went through some of the deepest, swampiest jungle where there were no paths ; suffering bleeding feet, loneliness and hunger, but all this he gladly endured for his new Master's sake.

We, as believers, all stopped complaining about the floods in Sena Madureira and the dirty river water that stained the walls so high in the church and house. Our God had a purpose in it all. Joao said he did not think he would ever have entered our church building in the town. The move to higher ground was surely the Lord's planning. So much happens in our lives which we count as disaster, and although we do not understand the reason at the time, afterwards we learn that it was our loving heavenly Father, Who in His love, planned it all.

Joao Marinho and his wife Maria were born and reared in Rio Grande do Norte, thousands of miles from the Acre Territory. His homeland was a place of earthquakes, drought and very little work. Joao had left these harsh circumstances along with many other men to find work cutting rubber trees in the forest around Sena Madureira. The life of the rubber cutters was hard and the wages minimal. Every day he left home for the plantation around 3.00 a.m. and returned in the afternoon around 4.00 p.m. for his main meal. Such was Joao's life on very low wages.

He and his wife Maria, built a small house in the forest. Maria had a very lonely life as she sat alone most of the day in that forest dwelling for she had no children at that time. Before Joao's conversion, instead of going home, he used to take the road to Sena Madureira where he would spend the evening and only arrive home around midnight. This lonely existence made Maria homesick for her family in Rio Grande do Norte. However, after Joao's conversion, their entire lives changed for the better. Maria started attending church with her husband, and soon afterwards, they moved into a house nearer town.

The floods finally receded and we were able to move back into our houses and into the church building in town. I bought some new boards, and the new kitchen was soon ready. We were all getting quite excited as we waited for the arrival of James and Dorrie. We heard they were now on a small slow launch making its way up river; we listened daily to hear the horn of the boat entering port.

As we waited, we were all amazed to see the wonderful changes God had worked in Joao Marinho's life. He was indeed a new creature in Christ Jesus. He travelled up and down the various rivers near to Sena and often made dangerous journeys overland into villages to tell others of his wonderful Saviour. This is the man the believers used to say was like Saul of Tarsus, hating Christians, now he was like Paul the Apostle seeking after the lost. Often he would sit and talk to me about the appalling need of his family back in Rio Grande do Norte in such superstition and darkness. How was he ever to reach them with the Gospel? We did not know at that time, but our dear Lord who saved Joao was silently planning it all.

How little did we think then that James and Dorrie Gunning, who were just about to arrive, would one day go with Joao to the distant Rio Grande do Norte and establish a pioneer work in the very village where Joao's family lived. God is faithful. Some of the early converts in that town were Joao's own family. His old father, over ninety years old, accepted the Lord Jesus as his Saviour. Joao would become the pastor of the churches in Campo Redondo and Malhada

Vermelha and today a growing church work continues to flourish in that area.

The following Sunday morning was beautiful, and just as the service was nearly finished, we heard the loud, sombre note of the horn announcing the arrival of the launch as it slowly approached our port after forty four days travelling on the River Purus. As the launch came nearer I could see James and Dorrie standing at the front waving to us. For them, this was the end of a long and wearisome journey. They told me afterwards they heard me shout "Hallelujah" as they disembarked.

I noticed, as they walked toward me, that Dorrie was limping. Then I noticed how badly her feet and ankles were swollen and inflamed. Yet they were so thankful to have arrived at their destination. They had endured forty eight days travelling on that launch with no comfort whatsoever. They had to sit in their hammocks by day and then sleep in them at night. There were no cabins on the boat, so the hammocks were slung anywhere and everywhere as darkness fell. It was at this hour the mosquitoes appeared in thousands for their daily feast.

Mosquito nets had been packed at the bottom of a trunk before leaving home and could not be found. Even if they had been found, there would have been no room for them on that small launch. One blessing was that the owner of the launch was a very nice young man who spoke English and did all he could to try to make them comfortable.

In Sena all the church members had waited after the service to greet the new missionaries, and what a welcome they gave them. After the initial greetings, we made our way to our small house. I had tried to make the house as nice as possible with a few curtains on the doors and some cushions on the wicker chairs I had bought in Manaus. The table was set for the longed for cup of tea and the tea set on the table was one of Dorrie's own wedding presents she had given me just after the war as I could not afford to buy one. After pulling off her white(or what had been white) shoes, dear Dorrie sat down and looked all around the small wooden house, now overcrowded with church members, and her first words were, "Why, this is just like home." This did prove to be home for James and Dorrie for more than forty years in the jungle and although they had no children, the dear Brazilians became their family.

Because they had arrived on the Lord's Day, they were given the opportunity to give their testimonies by interpretation in the evening Gospel service to a more than packed church. Very soon they began to participate in many of activities and meetings. At this same time many of the new converts were ready for baptism, and after a few months studying the language, James had the joy of baptizing them in a creek not far from the church.

Sometimes I think back to that Lord's day morning and the evening Gospel meeting in the dimly lit room of the makeshift church up the hill when Sena Madureira was flooded. I can still see the poor, misled and unhappy man sitting in the shadows at the back of the house listening to the sweetest story that ever was told - the story of Jesus and His love. I could not have thought or imagined that the same dear Joao Marinho would one day come to Belfast, Bangor and all over Northern Ireland to testify of what God had done in his life and through his work. He would also travel to Norway to do likewise. How good is the God we adore!

Farewell at Belfast Dock, 1937

With Willie, Margaret and Eleanor on our way home, 1946

*Sunday Morning Congregation at
Sena Madureira, Acre*

Church in Boca do Acre

Church and house in Sena Madureira

In Labrea

Morning Service, Sena Madureira Acre

Women's Meeting, Labrea

Women's Meeting, Boca do Acre

Deputation work

Field Conference, 1967

James and Dorrie Gunning

Our house, floods in Sena

Chapter Seven

❧

From Darkness To Light

In the interior towns of Brazil when a caller arrives at your front door they clap their hands to get your attention. There are no knockers on the doors nor are there door bells. As a midwife I was accustomed to hearing the clapping of hands at any hour of the night. One night around 11.00 p.m. I heard clapping at the front door. When I opened the door, two men were standing there. As I shone the torch light I could see they were dirty and dishevelled and very, very tired.

They said they had just arrived from a rubber plantation called Itapira; they had been carrying their father in a hammock since early morning, and they believed he was dying. They asked me to go and see him in the hospital. The hospital was a very basic building on the main road; it was furnished with a few iron beds and little else. The young woman in charge had very little nursing experience, but she was kind and did her best to make the patients comfortable as there was no doctor in the town.

When we got to the hospital, we found the old man crying out with pain. The nurse had already given him an injection to ease the pain and help him sleep, but he was still distressed. From my nursing training I recognized he had not long to live.

I tried to explain the way of salvation briefly and simply to the dear old man. I told him that our Saviour had suffered on the cross of Calvary to redeem him, and he only had to call on the Saviour and ask for forgiveness of his sins. I explained that the Lord would receive him and wash him in the soul cleansing blood and that very hour take him to his heavenly home. Alas, this old man could only reply, "My daughter, you have come too late," as he moaned in pain. He had never heard the way of salvation before, and, rejecting his only opportunity, he passed into a Godless eternity that night.

Four men carried the crude wooden coffin past our house the next morning on the way to the cemetery which was only a short distance up the road. Jose, his son, was too distraught to follow. He stood out on the road sobbing as if his heart would burst. Several times he cried out, "My father, my dear father, you did not do what the missionary asked you to do. Oh where are you now?"

I went out and brought Jose into the mission house and gave him some breakfast. He calmed down as we talked and I explained more fully to him the way of salvation. He wanted a Bible, but his most earnest request was for someone to visit his home at the rubber plantation. He said he had a very large room, and he promised to call his whole family and many neighbours to come and hear the gospel. He also promised to come and show us the way through the jungle when the date was arranged. I had to explain to Jose that a visit was not possible at that particular time but promised to make a date in the future.

I could not have gone right away because at that time we were awaiting the arrival of James and Dorrie Gunning coming for the first time from Northern Ireland, and there was much to do in preparation. The floods in our town of Sena Madureira had subsided and left the streets and houses in a terrible state. The church and our house were situated right on a corner at the lowest point in the town. Even though the house was built on stilts, every room was flooded. The small kitchen which had been about to fall into the flood water was being repaired by two workmen. Added to this, I was just recovering from malaria. I wanted everything ready for James and Dorrie's arrival and the dear Lord helped me in this every day.

Soon after James and Dorrie got settled into Sena the dry season was approaching and we made our plans for this promised visit to Jose's home on the rubber plantation in the depths of the jungle. We made the arrangements with Jose and he sent word to his family and friends.

This was James and Dorrie's first journey through the forest, and even with the beauty of God's creation all around us, it proved to be a long weary walk. We left the house at 7.00 a.m. with Jose leading the way. He set out at a fast walking pace in order to reach his house before the darkness invaded the forest at 5.30 p.m. We had a half an hour to stop at midday in an empty house. We gathered sticks and lit a fire to boil water for our tea, and I don't think tea ever tasted so nice and refreshing.

Jose had neglected to tell us of the bridges we would have to cross over on our way to the plantation. These bridges were large logs thrown across from one side of a creek to the other. There was no hand rail or even a rope to help us balance, and the logs were very wet and slippery. As if the effort to cross these logs was not bad enough, the men had to balance heavy loads on their backs.

They were carrying everything we needed for our short visit in water proof sacks which contained our hammocks, mosquito nets, a change of clothing in case it rained and, of course, a packet of tea! In many places the creeks were so full of raging and cascading streams that the water sometimes splashed over the makeshift bridge; in other places the water level was so low we dare not have looked down at the depth below us. One misplaced footstep would surely bring a terrible fall.

Many times on our journey through the jungle we said, "I can't do it," but with encouragement and help, we always managed to drag ourselves to our destination. How we thank our dear heavenly Father who was answering the petitions of so many faithful prayer partners as we made these journeys and arrived in safety.

On arrival at Jose's house we asked if we could wash before the meeting would begin. He very obligingly showed us a hole into which a trickle of muddy water was slowly running. At the first hole a few pigs were lying or wallowing in the surrounding mud. We were then directed to another hole where there was another small trickle of water. Turning a blind eye to the nearby pigs we washed our hands and faces and returned to Jose's house.

People started to arrive at the house from all different places. Some lived nearby while others had walked for hours and some of these with babies in their arms. Like ourselves, each person had brought his hammock and a change of clothing for an overnight stay. We were amazed to see the feast the family had provided for everybody in spite of the poor conditions in which they lived. Jose had killed a pig, a few chickens and some other meats from animals he had hunted in the forest. I could not help but think that God had provided a great feast for their hungering souls which was much more important. What an opportunity to teach these dear ones the Gospel for the very first time.

By the time everyone had finished eating and the people assembled for the meeting it was very late at night. There in the depths of the forest, with all the sounds of nocturnal life outside, in a dimly lit hut we began teaching them a simple chorus which they soon learned and then a verse from God's Word. Our voices seemed to echo from the surrounding jungle as if another voice was being heard. We do believe they heard God's voice at that simple meeting. After that we took time and explained the Gospel to them, Jose and his brother accepted the Lord Jesus as Saviour at their first hearing. It was well into the wee hours of the morning by the time the meeting finished, but we were glad to have been God's messengers to these forest dwellers.

The deep darkness of the early morning was well on us before we began to hang our hammocks from wall to wall. How that house took the strain of so many full hammocks suspended from it walls for the rest of the night, I will never know. The same God that made the walls of Jericho fall flat must have made those walls stand firm. Some of the travellers slept immediately being tired out from their journey. Others chatted all night amidst the coughing and crying from little babies. There was little sleep for us as I had to treat this one and that one for many varied ailments. At times we felt we needed some remedies ourselves.

Daylight seemed to come so early and for breakfast I've never seen so many eggs fried as again everybody was invited to eat. Following breakfast we had another meeting before we parted. We were amazed at how much they remembered from the previous night as we sang the choruses again and quoted God's Word. After giving a gospel lesson the people asked many questions. Soon we had to leave and make our long and exhausting trek back to Sena Madureira.

This was the first of many meetings we conducted in Itapira and as we continued to sow the Word of God many people trusted the Lord as their Saviour. Soon they built a simple but nice wee church near to the house where the first meetings began. When I came home on furlough, James and Dorrie continued to minister to these new converts. The journeys to Itapira never got any easier. Bridges still had to be crossed, hills had to be climbed and the pigs always shared the water holes. However, the treks were very worthwhile for many new names were written in the Lamb's Book of Life through the ministry of this small church over these many years.

Chapter Eight

✍

From Death's Door

One beautiful Sunday morning during spring in Sena Madureira, the church service was about to commence at 8.00 a.m. as usual. The church was already full of men, women and children, and we missionaries were making our way over from the Mission house nearby. Suddenly we were stopped by a man just at the veranda seeking our help. He told us that some of his relatives had arrived at his house after many days travelling with a little three year old girl who was very seriously ill with severe burns on both feet.

The story he told us was very sad. The girl's parents lived far up the river and a long way interior from the river bank. Besides cutting rubber on this remote plantation, year after year they used the ground around their forest home to plant various foods for the family. To help destroy weeds and flatten the earth, trees and undergrowth are cut down and set on fire. This fire smoulders for days; when it is cool, the replanting starts.

One morning the parents left home very early to go to work in the rice fields of another plantation. Soon their little girl missed them and ran outside crying for her parents. Sadly she did not know that the ground around the house was burning underneath the surface, and on her wee bare feet, she ran right through the smouldering, hot ashes. An older sister heard the terrible screaming, and realizing what had happened, immediately put on old shoes and went after the little one. Although she was not very old herself, she carried her sister all the way back to the house. As there was no way to get word to the parents, the child endured a long day of agony before the parents came back in the evening.

Faced with the terrible burns their little daughter had suffered they were not sure what to do. Local people, out of kindness and pity, tried in their simple ways to help the little girl. None of the primitive remedies seemed to help. Someone then suggested they should go to the missionaries. They immediately started out on the journey through the forest and down river to Sena Madureira. The journey took four days and when they arrived in town they came to see us. This was the story the man on the veranda told me as we hurried up hill that Sunday morning to see the child.

I remember going back to the Mission house that morning and packing the medical case with all I thought I would need. One thing I forgot were my medical gloves. As we came near the shack where the little girl was staying, the stench of decaying flesh was overwhelming, and the smell was much worse indoors. The parents were nice gentle folk and kept thanking me for coming. The dear wee girl had long since stopped crying. She was much too ill even to cry. As I carefully removed the dirty clothes which had been used as bandages, two little toes came off with the rags. I knew even before examining the leg that gangrene had set in. Although none of us were doctors, we knew that most advanced cases of gangrene require amputation. If the dead flesh was not removed, it could infect the entire body and soon cause death.

There was no doctor in Sena Madureira in those days, and we knew the little girl was at death's door. After removing the rotten flesh and cleaning the wounds, we endeavoured to treat her as best we could. We also prayed earnestly for the dear little girl and daily we saw that the Great Physician was answering our petitions. With daily treatment and continued prayer the little feet began to heal. The parents were very nice people and the mother said to me every day, "If your God heals my little daughter, I will become a Christian."

Not only did the Lord answer prayer in healing the little girl, but her mother did indeed accept the Lord Jesus Christ as Saviour. They stayed on in town and it was a joy to see the daughter not only attend the Sunday school, but also grow up to be a lovely young woman. She always had a slight limp, but every time I saw her I gave God the glory for her recovery. It was indeed a miracle.

The following Sunday I was suffering great pain in the thumb of my right hand. As the days passed the pain became more severe. With the increase of pain the thumb became swollen, inflamed and discoloured. Even penicillin had no effect on the infection.

We heard that a young doctor who had been visiting Sena, was at the airport awaiting a plane to take him to Rio Branco. James Gunning walked down to the riverside where the doctor was waiting and asked him to come to the house to see me. I noticed that he looked very concerned when he saw my thumb. Being an honest man and very frank, he told me the thumb did not look good. After examining it, he said he would stay in town and come the next morning and remove the nail.

True to his word, the doctor arrived early next morning; I was dreading the operation, but by this stage, the pain was so severe that anything would have been an improvement. The doctor began the operation by asking James to hold my wrist firmly with both hands as he made incisions and lifted off the nail. The pain was almost unbearable, but the worst was to come; I saw him break a very small vial and he told me this was going to hurt. Somehow I believed him because he had said nothing before hurting me the last time. I was right to believe him, for he proceeded to pour arsenic powder into the raw flesh from which he had removed the thumb-nail. It felt as if I were touching a red hot coal with my already painful thumb.

This treatment was repeated for three days after which I began to feel very ill with an onset of uncontrollable shivers. The doctor said he had done all he could and that I needed more specialized help than he could give. He told me to be ready early the next morning and when the plane arrived, he would take me to the hospital in Rio Branco.

I quickly packed a case, and in the morning I was at the airstrip by the river. James and Dorrie and some members of the church who had been praying for me came to see me off. Soon the plane arrived and taxied to where we were waiting. The doctor went on board first to explain the situation to the pilot. Even though the pilot saw me with my bandaged hand, he refused to take me on as he said the plane was already overloaded. With a sinking heart I watched my deliverance rise into the air without me and the hum of the plane drifted away into the haze of the horizon.

After the plane had disappeared, we all returned to the house wondering what we should do now. I knew the Lord was in control, and I trusted His divine omniscience in this matter. However, the pain was so intense, I found it hard to concentrate on anything else. God had His hand in all this.

James and Dorrie and the believers gathered around me. James laid his hand on my bandaged hand and prayed a prayer I will never forget; such peace came over us all. Surely this was a touch from our all seeing and Almighty Heavenly Father. We soon proved the Lord was working out His plan.

That same afternoon a man called at the door. He said he had been down at the air strip watching the plane and had seen that I had not got on board. He also heard that the pain in my thumb had got worse. The stranger said that he had been a nurse in the Brazilian army and had treated many others with the same condition. He named some injections which would cure and save my thumb. We soon got the prescribed medicines, and to my relief and our joy, after a short time, the healing began. Day by day I felt better, and slowly my thumb returned to its normal size and shape. After the ordeal was over, we could see that the Lord was the One who stepped in and prevented me from getting a seat on that plane.

Not long after this I was due to leave for furlough. Many believers came down to see me off on the small river steamer to Manaus. A tall well-dressed man came on board to say goodbye. Because he had been in the army for a number of years, we all called him "Captain." He certainly looked every bit a captain with his broad shoulders and straight back. He lifted my right hand and said as he shook it, "I have never been so glad to shake hands with anyone as I am today." I laughingly asked, "Why Captain? Are you glad to see me go?" "No, no," he replied, "not at all. The doctor who treated your thumb and wanted to take you to Rio Branco, told me that had you gone, it is very likely they would have amputated your thumb on arrival at the hospital."

With what joy and thanksgiving I was able to tell him that the Lord had prevented me from getting seat on the plane that day. I explained to him how when we came back to the house, we had committed the entire matter to the Lord in prayer. I then told him of the soldier coming to the house that very day and suggesting the injections which he had used in the army and the success that followed this treatment.

He was surprised to hear how these injections were so readily available in Sena. I further told him how that daily the pain subsided and slowly we saw the thumb heal and a new nail grow. The captain was amazed and said it was surely a miracle. I always felt it was a pity that the young doctor never heard how the Great Physician had looked after His own child.

"I the Lord thy God will hold thy right hand saying unto thee, Fear not; I will help thee." Isaiah 41:13

Chapter Nine

❧

From Sena To Boca do Acre

After working for four happy years in Sena Madureira I returned to Northern Ireland. James and Dorrie were well settled into the work and had a very full programme of meetings, visitation etc. Dorrie was greatly involved in midwifery and it was proving a useful key in the work. The Lord was blessing so abundantly on Sunday mornings that the people packed the church. The blessing was not only confined to the church. We were also seeing God change people's lives in the interior villages deep into the surrounding forest. To help James and Dorrie in the work there had arrived a new missionary, Jack Finlay, a young man from Belfast.

Many of the believers, living in the interior villages, had built small churches in which they met on the Lord's Day and during the week for prayer and Bible study. These small churches were simple in construction as were most interior houses. Rough boards formed the walls half way up, and the top half was open. the rustic structures were covered over with a thatched roof which consisted mostly of palm leaves and straw which had been gathered from the forest. Although the surroundings were quite primitive, the meetings were always blessed with a real sense of the Lord's presence. On

Sundays, when the believers were remembering our dear Lord and Saviour at the Communion Supper, one of the missionaries would undertake the long walk through the forest to join in their special service.

While we continued working in Sena Madureira, the Lord laid on our hearts a great burden for a town away down the river Purus and at the mouth of the river Acre. The town was Boca do Acre which literally means "the mouth of the Acre." I had first seen Boca do Acre while travelling from Manaus to Rio Branco with the McCombs in 1937. The boat on which we were travelling stopped there for several days. With time to spare, we had decided to walk up the main street, and Willie McComb distributed gospel literature. He had begun talking to a man and asked him if he knew of anyone in the town who had a Bible. After thinking for a moment, the man told us of a woman called Dona Nene Jacinto who "believed in something like that." He told us where Dona Nene lived and we went to visit her .

She was thrilled to meet us and although she did not have a Bible, she had a well worn page from a hymn book. She treasured this, and whenever one of her friends died, she would go to the funeral and read from this page. Her husband was Syrian, and he made us feel very welcome in his home. Sr. Jacinto agreed to let us conduct a gospel meeting in his home, and although the front room was filled with great balls of rubber and sacks of Brazil nuts which were waiting to be shipped down river, the people managed to crowd in to the confined space. However, since that meeting, there had been no ongoing witness for Christ in Boca do Acre.

The town itself was not very big, but it was a busy junction as the boats from Bolivia came down the river Acre. Also, all the boats coming from the Amazon area of Peru, come down the river Purus heavily laden with cargo, and meet at Boca do Acre. I can remember standing on the river bank at Boca do Acre and seeing the river mouth fill up with boats from Brazil, Bolivia and Peru.

Many different types of goods were brought past this town. The necessities of life were brought to the dwellers of the region from other parts of Brazil and these were sold and exchanged for the raw materials of the forest. The most common of these included timber from the forest, great balls of crude and raw rubber from the cutter's plantations, Brazil nuts and jaguar skins. Some of the boats would return to unload their cargos in Manaus, fifteen hundred miles away, while others navigated all the way to Belem, which was another thousand miles down river. The raw materials were then exported to various parts of the world.

The Boca do Acre, being the port where boats from all parts docked, was the centre of entertainment for the crews for several days during their short stays in the town. One of the favourite pastimes was drinking as there was always plenty of cheap liquor for sale in the shanty bars. This, coupled with the gambling, prostitution and other vices which often resulted in gun fights or knifings, earned the town the reputation of being called "the Devil's Den."

The burden for this town grew heavier as James and Dorrie and Jack Finlay prayed about its needs. One day while James was having his quiet time of devotions, the Lord spoke clearly to him as he had been praying about moving down river to the Boca do Acre. The verse God used to speak to him was Acts 18:9-10, "Then spake the Lord to Paul in the night by a vision, 'Be not afraid, but speak, and hold not thy peace;

for I am with thee, and no man shall set on thee to hurt; for I have much people in this city.'" Here at last was God's call.

As soon as Sander Tonnenson, the Norwegian missionary, returned from furlough with his young wife, Ingrid, God showed them very clearly that they should take over the work in Sena Madureira and the surrounding areas.

It was in 1952 that James and Dorrie Gunning left Sena and travelled down river to Boca do Acre to find a house in which they could live. Because there were few houses available, humanly speaking it would have been difficult to find a place. God answered prayer, and just as He had opened a door to go so we knew He would provide a home in which to stay. Sure enough, they acquired a large roomy house which was offered to them for rent. Very soon James was able to purchase some furniture for the kitchen, a table and chairs and soon the house was liveable.

By the time I had returned from furlough, the work in the town was well under way. The missionaries had secured a house which a couple opened for the meetings at the far end of the street from which they had their accommodation. As the numbers grew, the couple gladly took away a dividing wall between their sitting room and kitchen to make room for more people. In that house many souls were won for Christ, including Sr. Jacinto and many of his eight children.

Facing this house was a site just large enough on which to build a church. Although we were able to buy the site, there was no money to buy building supplies or to employ workers to build the church. However, the Lord had planned all of this long before and had given James and Jack the abilities and knowledge to build this church. James and Jack took a large canoe down river, walked into the forest looking out for the best trees from which to saw wooden planks for the church.

I do not think many people reading this will fully appreciate the time, sweat and many weeks of labour that were expended by Jack and James in this hard work. After selecting the tree and chopping it down, they tied thick ropes around their waists, attached the ropes to the tree trunks and then pull them to a especially erected platform on which they suspended the logs. They then started to saw them into planks using a double-handed wood-cutter's saw. Jack stood on the top of the platform, and James stood on the ground . They worked the saw up and down for hours each day. After several boards were produced, they were brought to the side of the river and then down the steep bank to be loaded into the canoe. After the canoe was filled, they had to paddle back to town. The boards were left to dry and then would follow the planing of the boards before using them in the building of the church. This was their daily task for several months, and being heavy and dangerous work, Dorrie must have been glad to see them home safely each evening .

Jack and James not only built the church in this manner, but also a very nice pulpit, communion table and comfortable pews. After a lot of hard work the church building was completed and the date set for the opening. The official opening was held one Saturday afternoon after I arrived and I was delighted to meet the new converts who had been won to the Lord while I was away. The church was built right at the side of the river, overlooking the port where all the boats docked. James saw this as a way to witness and a large text from God's Word was displayed at the back of the building for all to see.

My second term at the Boca do Acre began when I arrived back just before Christmas, 1953. I was welcomed by my colleagues and we sat talking throughout Christmas Eve night drinking tea and catching up on news of all the happenings since I had left.

They told me how the Lord had saved many souls. The outreach had also been extended to Terra Firme on the other side of town where meetings were conducted in various houses. To get there the missionaries had to cross a treacherous stretch of the fast flowing river and then climb a muddy and slippery bank until they came to wooden steps with seventy eight wooden rungs. In the tropical sunshine, this was an exhausting journey and we found it necessary to stop periodically to catch a breath of air and have a look at the surrounding jungle.

Many at Terra Firme had trusted the Lord and as they grew in the faith, they made the effort of coming over to the regular meetings conducted in the church at Boca do Acre on the Lord's Day and during the week. They were so eager to learn God's Word that they were prepared to face the dangers of crossing this perilous stretch of the river.

As increasing numbers of believers came, James found an answer to their problem. A house right at the top of the steep ascent at Terra Firme became vacant and James bought it. With the help of the believers they soon transformed it into a meeting place; in fact it was ready for use the day after he bought it. The purchase of this house aroused the anger of a local cleric who vowed that he would personally see that the doors of the new evangelical church never opened. In opposition the cleric actually bought the house next to the church to start novenas in that house.

After chatting all through that Christmas Eve night when I had just arrived, we opened the shutters early to find the sunlight already streaming through the trees and trying to find a way into the house. We looked up the street and realised something was wrong. People were running past our house crying; others were being carried , and it was apparent they had been injured. We thought it strange that no one had asked the missionaries for help as we were usually the first ones called in any medical emergency.

We later learned that during the midnight mass on Christmas Eve there had been a terrible accident at the Catholic Church. In order to accommodate the expected crowds at the mass, they had built a balcony in the church. It was erected in a hurry, and unfortunately, it collapsed under the weight of the crowds that gathered in. The priest, who was leading the proceedings, was on the ground floor just under where the balcony fell. He was seriously injured and had to be transported to the south of Brazil for special treatment. We were speechless when we heard the news, for he was the very man who threatened us and vowed that our little church at Terra Firme would never open.

When we officially opened the small church at Terra Firme later that Christmas Day, the believers gathered and brought many interested friends. James commenced the proceedings by praying for the salvation of those who had been injured and especially for the priest who had already gone on the long journey to seek treatment. It was a memorable service, and we gave thanks to God for this new place in which to preach and teach the Gospel of Jesus Christ.

Not long after our opening service, a very frightening experience happened in which the Lord thwarted the Prince of Darkness once again. The house which had become our new home at Boca do Acre had three front windows which offered a fine view of the river. During the rainy season when the river was flooding, we were able to watch the large boats going up river to Rio Branco and some on to Bolivia.

Early one morning two large boats arrived and docked on the other side of the river. This was a welcome sight in any port as they usually sold biscuits and other luxury items not normally available in these interior towns.

On this morning we coaxed James into taking us over to the boats to look for biscuits or onions, and even though he was busy, he agreed. Our large canoe with an outboard motor was always kept tied up outside our front door during the flood. We all got into the canoe and went laden with gospel tracts in Portuguese to give to the crews on the boats.

Not only had I just arrived back from furlough, but James, Dorrie and Jack were preparing to leave for theirs. All in all, there were six missionaries in the canoe. Besides James, Dorrie and Jack Finlay, Jack and Joan Mawdsley who had not long arrived in Brazil, and myself, were all on board. As we moved out from the shore and into the middle of the river, we felt the strong current pulling us down river. James had to increase the throttle, but even this was not enough as the current swept us down river past the large boats as we tried to ease the canoe closer to the boats to let us disembark.

Another large canoe which was tied securely to the side of one of the boats, was blocking our approach. As the two canoes came closer to each other James fought to swing the front of our canoe back toward the middle of the river, but his efforts were in vain. With an ugly thud the two canoes came together, and because we were so heavily loaded, our canoe was pushed down into the river. The muddy brown water gushed into the canoe adding to the confusion. Somehow, as the canoe started to go down the other missionaries were able to scramble to the nearby boats or jump over board and some crew members dragged them on to the decks of the docked boats. They were soaked and shocked and Dorrie fainted. Her legs and body were badly bruised.

I had been sitting at the prow of the canoe, and the force of the impact threw me forward. I just faintly remember catching hold of the wheel, my handbag still on my arm. As the cold, strong fingers of the current grasped me, I prayed to God for deliverance. Witnesses said that our boat disappeared below the two other boats. The people said they were sure I was lost. My missionary colleagues were stunned. Although they had been delivered from a watery grave they were in distress for they also thought I had drowned in the submerged canoe.

Down river at the confluence of the rivers Purus and Acre is a dangerous spot where, because of the raging currents, many lives have been lost. Everybody was sure I was another victim of this treacherous river. After what seemed an age, in the mercy of the Lord, the prow of our canoe came into view above the water on the far side of the two boats. Although dazed and feeling I had been to the grave and back, I was still holding on to the wheel with my handbag still on my arm! Just at the same time, an old man travelling in his canoe spotted me. He hurried over near to our emerging canoe, shouting at me to come to him, but I did not know how I was able to go to him. Another man came to the first man's aid and together they pulled me from the dangerous current into their canoe. I felt as though a miracle had taken place and immediately I thanked God for His deliverance.

As I came ashore I must have looked a terrible sight. I had lost my shoes, my long hair was hanging around my face, I was shivering with shock, but my handbag was still safely tucked under my arm! I was told that if I had let go the wheel I would most certainly have drowned. However, I was sure that it was not my holding onto the wheel that had saved me, rather it was our wonderful Lord holding unto me.

Crowds from the town had gathered on the river bank to see the outcome of the frightening experience. Many said they had been praying for us in those awful moments. God hears the prayers of His children. Since we had not been in Boca do Acre very long, we felt this accident was an attack of evil on the new work on the "Devil's Den."

Surely the word given to Paul at Corinth, and given to James before he left Sena Madureira, proved to be true. "Be not afraid, but speak and hold not thy peace, for I am with thee, and no man shall set on thee to hurt thee, for I have much people in this city." All that the Lord had promised had been fulfilled.

Chapter Ten

❧

From The Terror Of The Whirlwind

For many weeks we had been praying about making a visit to Monte Verde, a place far down river from Boca do Acre. This was the home of some civilized Indians of the Apauani tribe, who needed to hear the gospel message. The last time we visited them they had given us a noisy reception. All the men wanted to talk at the same time while dogs barked out the news that strangers were in the area. We wondered if they had heard anything we said or if they could possibly remember the Scripture verse we had tried to teach them.

James, Dorrie, Fred Orr and I, along with a believer from the church, set out to make further contact with them. After the canoe journey down river, we climbed the steep bank and then walked through the forest to arrive at their village.

Their houses were small, constructed of rough logs from the forest and covered with palm leaves. They seemed pleased to see us, and the chief and his wife were very friendly and invited us to have something to eat with them. They served us strange looking soup and little pieces of meat, which, no doubt, they had hunted in the forest. They sat and watched us as we ate what they had provided.

After our meal, we conducted an outdoor meeting, and quite a number gathered round to listen to us and to sing "At the Cross, at the Cross, where I first saw the light" and other rousing gospel hymns. They listened attentively, unlike the last occasion. They seemed to be pondering the message about the Saviour who loved them enough to die for them. Later on, after we promised them another visit, James commended them to the Lord in prayer, and we then set out on our homeward journey.

As we walked the forest path back to the our canoe, we felt as happy as the numerous birds in the trees sounded as they sang praises to the Creator, and we were encouraged at having such an effective contact with these dear people. We knew our friends back at the Boca church were praying for us.

Suddenly as we walked down to our canoe, we noticed that the birds had ceased their singing, and there was an eerie, heavy feeling in the air. The cool breeze which had felt so refreshing in the summer heat had now become a wind which blew towering dark clouds closer and closer. Soon these sombre clouds rolled overhead hiding the sun. We rushed down the steep bank to the canoe where we dropped wearily down on the hard bench. We were thankful for the rest after having been on our feet all day. As Fred started the motor, he kept one eye on the turbulent sky and remarked that the dark clouds seemed to be following us. We were soon travelling up river as fast as the motor would take us, but it was not long before we noticed that we were the only boat left on the river. All the larger boats had tied up at the port on the other side of the river.

Just as we were contemplating making for the river bank, the black clouds seemed to drop from the sky and envelope the canoe, the river, and all living things. Suddenly, like a rag doll in the hand of an ill-tempered child, the canoe was violently thrown from side to side. Abruptly, the straining motor hesitated then coughed and died. We were now completely helpless as we had no power to direct the canoe. It seemed we were at the mercy of the wind and waves. We felt the canoe being spun round and round as the current and the wind battled for supreme control. Because of the wind-driven rain, we could not see where we headed or if anything was coming toward us.

As we held on to each other (and anything within reach), I thought that this must be similar to what the disciples experienced on the Sea of Galilee long ago when Jesus calmed the sea with a simple command. But my mind soon returned to the situation at hand as the canoe was quickly filling with water both from the rain and the waves which were washing over the sides. Large hail stones were pelting down on us, the pain felt from the wind-driven ice seemed like needles being stuck into us. As death stared us in the face, like the disciples we cried to the Lord for help.

Soon the wind began to abate and the rain to slacken. As the clouds, borne on by the wind rushed away up river, we were able to see around us and we knew that God had calmed the waters once again. Somehow we were able to get the canoe into the side of the river bank. James and Fred tried to start the out-board motor again, but without success. By this time it was getting late, and we felt very isolated in the impending darkness. Dorrie and I decided to walk through the forest while the men continued working on the motor. Eventually we heard the putt-putt of the motor bringing the canoe around the bend of the river, and before long James and Fred caught up with us. Once again we lowered our weary bodies onto the hard benches for the final stretch of our journey to Boca do Acre .

When we arrived in Boca do Acre we saw the damage that this tropical whirlwind had done to the wooden structures in the town. Roofs had been ripped off and in some instances, entire houses had been torn apart. We were thankful that God had preserved our lives. The badly shaken believers were glad to see us back home safely. They told us they had been praying for us.

On arrival at our house we took time to clean up and change into fresh clothes before gathering round the table to thank our heavenly Father for the great deliverance. We read Psalm 126:2-3; "Then was our mouth filled with laughter, and our tongue with singing; then said they among the heathen, the Lord hath done great things for them. The Lord hath done great things for us whereof we are glad." We rejoiced as we considered how the evil one had been defeated once again.

Some months after this experience we received a letter from two prayer partners in Belfast. One afternoon while they were sitting at their fireside knitting, they felt constrained to pray for us. They were greatly burdened and knelt by their chairs and committed us to the Lord. Our dear heavenly Father had heard and answered their prayers.

David Livingstone wrote home on one occasion stating, "I can do without your money; I can live without your letters; but I must have your prayers."

Chapter Eleven

From A Seed To A Harvest

As I returned from furlough in 1954 I did not go back to Sena Madureira but to Boca do Acre, the town where a new work had begun. James and Dorrie Gunning and Jack Finlay were due to leave for a needed furlough so early in that year they went to Manaus. They were anxious to be there for the arrival of Fred and Ina Orr who were travelling to Brazil by boat from Liverpool.

When he was a teenager, Fred signed as a professional footballer in Belfast. It was in the midst of his football career that he trusted the Lord Jesus as his Saviour. Ina also was a Christian and they both joined their lives in marriage to serve the Lord wherever God would indicate. They were greatly used of God in Northern Ireland. Besides many opportunities for Gospel campaigns and preaching engagements, Fred led Mr. Sam Doherty to faith in Christ and then introduced Sam and Sadie Doherty to the work of Child Evangelism Fellowship. That was to develop into the establishing of the C.E.F. in United Kingdom and then throughout Europe.

Not content with a good home and a secure standard of living, Fred and Ina felt God was calling them to the regions beyond in spite of many opportunities for Christian service at home. After training in Glasgow they were accepted by the Acre Gospel Mission. On 15th. March, 1954 they sailed to Brazil.

James and Dorrie had been working in the interior for five years. The few weeks spent in Manaus while they waited for the Fred and Ina brought a welcome rest before sailing for home on the same boat on which the new couple were due to arrive.

Willard and Grace Stull, American Baptist missionaries in Manaus and good friends of our missionaries, kindly prepared a room in their home for the new couple from Northern Ireland. This was a lovely welcome for Fred and Ina after travelling for more than a month on the Booth Line steamer. They had crossed the Atlantic and now the same boat had brought them 1,000 miles up the great Amazon river. To meet three missionaries from Belfast was a great blessing to them and the few days together were very precious. James and Dorrie soon left for Ireland and Jack Finlay went off to be married to an American missionary in United States.

I wrote to Fred and Ina in Manaus and told them that all was ready for their arrival in Boca do Acre. They replied telling me that they were having difficulty securing passages on the small Catalina amphibian plane to take them to the Boca. At times they were offered one place only but, understandably, they wanted to travel together on the same flight for the long journey.

Just then they got word that a very good boat was leaving Manaus for Labrea, which was about the half way point of journey to Boca do Acre. At Labrea they would then change to a smaller boat, a paddle steamer, locally known as a "chata", for the remainder of the trip. This was the usual way for the Acre missionaries to travel these long distances.

Our friend Willard Stull booked the passages for Fred and Ina for their first trip interior. During their stay in Manaus the newly arrived young couple had endeared themselves to many of the members at Willard's church. Ina was a trained singer and had learned enough Portuguese in Manaus to enable her to sing solos at the Sunday evening services. With the aid of a loudspeaker the whole district could hear this sweet voice singing the Gospel hymns. The Church had a wonderful "send off" and strange as it may seem, on that last Sunday night Ina sang "The Holy City." How significant this would prove to be.

Is it any wonder that these same people in Manaus would be stunned when, within a week of leaving them, they would hear that Ina had passed into the presence of her Lord on the very river steamer on which they had left?

Taking their leave from Manaus on the river boat, they proceeded up the great Solimoes river and then entered into the river Purus along the banks of which most of the work of the Mission would centre. On board the boat Ina won the hearts of many and the captain was like a father to both Fred and Ina and they spent hours on the bridge trying to speak to him in Portuguese.

Fred and Ina could not have imagined what those crucial days would hold for them and the inhabitants of that region. Just after they had entered the river Purus and almost two days into the journey, Ina felt unwell. Although she had taken every precaution against sickness, it seemed a mystery how she had become ill. Besides giving her medicines, Fred earnestly prayed for the Lord to preserve her life. God had other plans.

Ina was ill for only five days. During that time she never slept and Fred seldom left her side - great grace and strength must have been given him from our heavenly Father. No one on board the boat knew a word of English to speak a word of comfort or cheer to the young couple. The boat docked at Canutama and Fred sought in vain for medical help in that small town. Slowly the boat made its way further up river to Labrea bearing the young couple to a forlorn hope of some medical assistance in that town. Just as the river slowly ebbed its way to the great sea, so Ina's life slowly ebbed into the great eternity.

It was on Friday 4th. June 1954 that Ina went to be with her Lord. Early that day she joined Fred as he prayed and asked God to forgive him for doubting God's promises. At 6.00 p.m. she became delirious and by 8.00 p.m. she went to be with her Saviour. Fred, as he had been since she became ill, was at her side. She was only twenty nine years old. Such a short life and yet the impact of that life would be inestimable. Fred was left stunned and shocked. He had come to serve the Lord. He was far from home and far from any colleagues and in the company of strangers whose language he did not know and with whom he could communicate very little. Often when I thought of these circumstances I would recall how David Livingstone buried his wife in the heart of Africa. The great difference was that David Livingstone could speak the language of the people with whom he worked. Fred and Ina were barely five weeks in Brazil, he did not know the language, he had no Christians with him and no colleagues nearby.

On Saturday some local men dug a grave in a little cemetery on the outskirts of this previously unknown town called Labrea. Under the intense heat of the tropical sun they lowered Ina's coffin into the grave. It was a heartbreaking moment. Fred read Psalm 23 at the graveside and committed the remains of his dear wife to the soil of Brazil, the land in which they had come to serve the Lord. Fred could not have known how precious a seed had been sown that day.

When he returned to the boat he was distraught and yet he had an unusual peace. His mind was with Ina's parents and his own family at home and how they would receive the news. The nightmare experience of the last five days flooded in on him. He also wondered how he would travel to the Boca or should he return to Manaus. In this perturbed state he happened to glance at his Bible and he could only see one verse standing out in bold print, "Jesus said unto him, 'What I do thou knowest not now; but thou shalt know hereafter." (John 13:7) Besides God's peace, Fred sensed the assurance of the Lord's presence in a particularly real way.

Meanwhile, the believers at the Boca do Acre were planning a Welcome Service for the new couple arriving from Northern Ireland. The Sunday School children were to sing as a choir. The elders and deacons had planned to say a few words of welcome and I was to translate into English for Fred and Ina.

Senhor Davi Salgado, a Jew who lived in Boca do Acre, had a shop in town. He came one day to tell me he was going down river on a small boat to meet up with the larger steamer returning to Manaus. He knew about the new missionary couple arriving in Manaus and their plans to come to the Boca do Acre. He said he would be meeting the young couple on their way through. I had already received letters from Belfast addressed to Fred and Ina and Davi said he would be glad to take them down river and give the correspondence to them. I also wrote a letter to Fred and Ina and told them all was in readiness for their arrival.

On the Saturday morning an old man came to the door of the Mission house. He said he had come from the telegraph radio station where they operated in morse code high up on the hill on the other side of the river. He handed me a piece of paper and when I unfolded it these are the words I read, "The missionary Ina Orr died on board this boat last night at Labrea. Please contact husband to arrange about burial." The radio operator sent word to say this was the message he had received from Labrea and he requested that I accompany the old man to the station as he wanted to speak with me.

To this day I do not remember crossing the river and climbing that hill. On arrival at the telegraph station I could only write out the message to Fred, word by word in English. The operator transmitted the message as I had written it, "Lay Ina to rest in Labrea and come to Boca do Acre." Within a short time I received a reply which said, "Coming on plane tomorrow, Sunday."

My Jewish friend, Davi Salgado was in Labrea when these sad events occurred and he was such a help and comfort to Fred. He had carried Fred's Bible to the cemetery while Fred shouldered the coffin. He said that just when Fred had finished reading from the Bible at the grave side, a beautiful rainbow appeared. Fred pointed to the rainbow and then to the Bible and then directed his pointing finger to the grave. Davi was very touched as were the many Brazilians around the grave.

The captain of the boat was a very helpful man and had done all he could for Ina. After she died he sat up all night on the deck with Fred and did not leave his side until Fred embarked on the Catalina plane that would bring him to Boca do Acre.

When he arrived at the Boca Fred was utterly exhausted. Only the Lord knew how deep were the waters of sorrow through which he was passing. We sat and talked and I tried to be a good listener for him. Some days after his arrival his baggage also came on a river boat. He was not interested in unpacking what he and Ina had packed in Northern Ireland before they left for Brazil. I had to go through all their belongings and keep out what belonged to Fred. The opening of each case was a painful exercise.

Fred applied himself to master the Portuguese language and very soon he was speaking very well. The people at the Boca do Acre loved him and being aware of his circumstances they sought to express their sympathy and support. However, Fred felt he wanted to go down to Labrea and erect something at Ina's grave.

When he got there he was more fluent in the language. In spite of the fact that Labrea was the centre for the Catholic church for all the river Purus, he found there was not only a great expression of love from a lot of the people, but also, he discovered there was a tremendous need for a Gospel witness in Labrea. Prior to Fred and Ina arriving in Labrea the Bishop had written a short history of the town in which he boasted that evangelicals had never come to Labrea. They had now arrived, but not in the way we might have planned.

After James and Dorrie Gunning returned from furlough they left Boca do Acre to go and help Fred establish a witness in Labrea. A Syrian man who lived in Labrea had become a very good friend to Fred and gave him a prime piece of ground near to the centre of town. James and Fred worked hard to erect a beautiful wooden house which was used both as a residence and a meeting place on the large veranda. Contacts were made with the neighbours and people in the town. Soon meetings were started and many men, women and children heard the Gospel for the first time and quite a few of them came to the Lord.

Some years later, a lovely church was built at the side of the Mission house and on the same ground that the Syrian friend had given years ago. Also on the same piece of ground a Christian School was built. The Church which has a capacity for three hundred people, is well filled and has a Brazilian pastor. The School is staffed with Christian teachers and has over two hundred children attending each day.

Ina Orr did not die in vain. On her gravestone Fred had inscribed in English the text from John 17:4, "I have glorified Thee on earth. I have finished the work which Thou gavest me to do." How fitting these words are. Ina's life was given in sacrifice to obey Christ's command "Go ye into all the world and preach the Gospel." God saw that her work was finished and planted her remains in the soil of a town in the heart of the Amazon. That was the very seed that God would use to bring a bountiful harvest.

More than forty years later, Fred Orr is still in Brazil serving the Lord. Recently the Labrea Town Council honoured Fred at a special meeting at the Town Hall and conferred on him the freedom of the town.

The events of those sorrowful days of June 1954 are not only an unforgettable memory, they also embody the challenge to all our missionaries serving the Lord in various countries today . "*He that goeth forth and weepeth, bearing precious seed, shall doubtless come again with rejoicing bringing his sheaves with him.* "

There is no gain but by a loss,
We only conquer through the Cross;
The corn of wheat to multiply,
Must fall into the ground and die.
O, should a soul alone remain
When it a hundredfold can gain?

Our souls are held by what they hold;
Slaves still are slaves in chains of gold:
To whatsoever we may cling,
We make it a soul-chaining thing,
Whether it be a life or land,
And dear as our right eye or hand

Whenever you ripe fields behold,
Waving to God their sheaves of gold,
Be sure some corn of wheat has died,
Some saintly soul been crucified:
Someone has suffered, wept and prayed,
And fought hell's legions undismayed!

~ A. S. Booth-Clibborn.